AMAZING INVENTIONS
VIDEO GAMES
A GRAPHIC HISTORY

SEAN TULIEN
ILLUSTRATED BY **DAVID M. BUISÁN**

Graphic Universe™ • Minneapolis

Graphic Universe™
An imprint of Lerner Publishing Group, Inc.
241 First Avenue North
Minneapolis, MN 55401 USA

For reading levels and more information, look up this title at www.lernerbooks.com.

Main body text set in CCHedgeBackwards 7/9
Typeface provided by Comicraft.

Library of Congress Cataloging-in-Publication Data

Names: Tulien, Sean, writer. | Buisán, David M., illustrator.
Title: Video games : a graphic history / written by Sean Tulien ; illustrated by David Buisán.
Description: Minneapolis : Graphic Universe, [2021] | Series: Amazing inventions | Includes bibliographical references and index. | Audience: Ages 8–12 | Audience: Grades 4–6 | Summary: "Video games evolved from simple consoles to cutting-edge home entertainment to some of the world's most popular apps. Find out more about the technological innovations, major players, and controversies that have made video-game history"— Provided by publisher.
Identifiers: LCCN 2020006427 (print) | LCCN 2020006428 (ebook) | ISBN 9781541581500 (library binding) | ISBN 9781728417486 (ebook)
Subjects: LCSH: Video games—History—Comic books, strips, etc.—Juvenile literature. | Technological innovations—Juvenile literature. | Graphic novels.
Classification: LCC GV1469.3 .T85 2021 (print) | LCC GV1469.3 (ebook) | DDC 794.8—dc23

LC record available at https://lccn.loc.gov/2020006427
LC ebook record available at https://lccn.loc.gov/2020006428

Manufactured in the United States of America
3 - 52204 - 47960 - 11/19/2021

TABLE OF CONTENTS

CHAPTER 1

A LITTLE BROWN BOX TO *FORTNITE*

ON JULY 28, 2019, 16-YEAR-OLD GAMER KYLE "BUGHA" GIERSDORF WON A $3 MILLION GRAND PRIZE IN THE FORTNITE WORLD CUP. ABOUT TWO MILLION PEOPLE WATCHED THE EVENT LIVE.

IT'S JUST ABSOLUTELY UNREAL!

HOW DID VIBRANT VIDEO GAMES LIKE FORTNITE . . .

. . . EVOLVE FROM A LITTLE BOX?

IN THE 1960S, AN ENGINEER NAMED RALPH BAER WORKED FOR SANDERS ASSOCIATES IN NEW HAMPSHIRE.

WHILE THERE, HE BUILT THE FIRST VIDEO GAME CONSOLE PROTOTYPE BETWEEN 1967 AND 1968.

THE JOYSTICK CONTROLLER BAER CREATED REMAINS PART OF MOST MODERN VIDEO GAME CONTROLLERS.

THERE IS A HORIZONTAL KNOB HERE . . . WHEN I TWIDDLE IT, IT MOVES MY PADDLE FROM LEFT TO RIGHT. THERE'S ALSO A VERTICAL CONTROL, WHICH MOVES MY PADDLE UP AND DOWN.

BAER LATER SAID OF HIS INVENTION, "LITTLE DID I KNOW THAT I HAD STARTED THE BALL ROLLING ON SOMETHING MUCH BIGGER . . . THAN ANYONE COULD HAVE IMAGINED AT THE TIME."

BAER CALLED HIS CREATION THE "BROWN BOX." THE SYSTEM WAS BASIC. BUT IT WAS THE BIRTH OF SOMETHING MAJOR!

TELEVISION INSPIRED BAER. BY THE 1960S, TVS HAD BECOME PART OF MANY AMERICAN HOUSEHOLDS. WITH BAER'S BROWN BOX, PEOPLE COULD PLAY GAMES ON THEIR TVS.

UGH. YOU WON AGAIN.

OKAY!

BEST THREE OUT OF FIVE?

IN 1972, MAGNAVOX COMPANY BEGAN TO MAKE AND SELL BAER'S INVENTION. THEY GAVE IT A NEW NAME: THE ODYSSEY. A PING-PONG GAME WAS ONE OF SEVERAL OFFERED ON THE SYSTEM. THE ODYSSEY WAS AN EXCITING NEW FORM OF ENTERTAINMENT. HOWEVER, SOME PEOPLE THINK IT WASN'T THE FIRST OF ITS KIND.

BAER CREATED HIS BROWN BOX IN 1968. TEN YEARS EARLIER, PHYSICIST WILLIAM HIGINBOTHAM INTRODUCED THE GAME TENNIS FOR TWO TO THE PUBLIC.

UNLIKE BAER'S INVENTION, HIGINBOTHAM'S GAME DID NOT USE A VIDEO SCREEN (SUCH AS A TV SCREEN). USERS PLAYED TENNIS FOR TWO ON AN OSCILLOSCOPE. THIS IS A LAB INSTRUMENT THAT SHOWS MATHEMATICAL MODELS SUCH AS GRAPHS.

IT'S ELECTRONIC TENNIS!

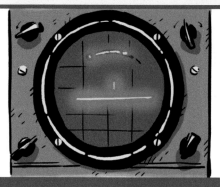

HIGINBOTHAM CREATED AN ELECTRONIC GAME. BUT BECAUSE IT DIDN'T USE A VIDEO SCREEN, NOT EVERYONE CONSIDERS IT THE FIRST VIDEO GAME.

EVEN SO, MOST PEOPLE AGREE THAT BOTH INVENTORS TOOK IMPORTANT STEPS IN BRINGING VIDEO GAMES TO LIFE.

BAER FACED MORE THAN CONTROVERSY. HE HAD COMPETITION TOO!

THE SAME YEAR MAGNAVOX RELEASED THE ODYSSEY, NOLAN BUSHNELL AND TED DABNEY FOUNDED VIDEO GAME COMPANY ATARI. WITH ENGINEER ALLAN ALCORN, THEY CREATED THE ARCADE GAME PONG.

PONG WAS SIMILAR TO BAER'S PING-PONG GAME. BUT, PEOPLE PLAYED PONG ON LARGER MACHINES IN PUBLIC PLACES. PLAYERS HAD TO INSERT MONEY BEFORE STARTING A GAME.

OOH, TOUGH LUCK.

SOMEONE GET MORE QUARTERS!

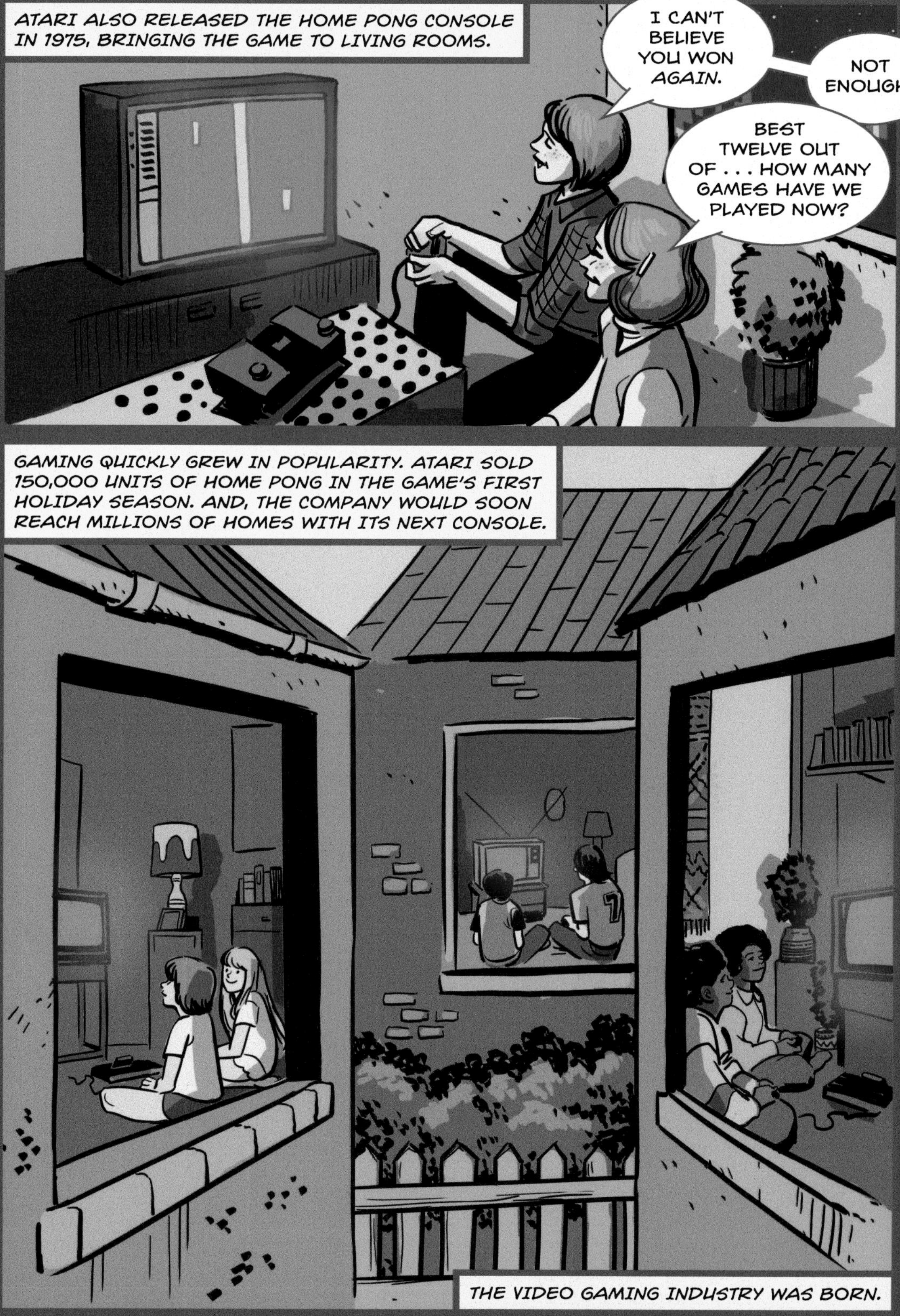
ATARI ALSO RELEASED THE HOME PONG CONSOLE IN 1975, BRINGING THE GAME TO LIVING ROOMS.
I CAN'T BELIEVE YOU WON AGAIN.
NOT ENOUGH!
BEST TWELVE OUT OF . . . HOW MANY GAMES HAVE WE PLAYED NOW?
GAMING QUICKLY GREW IN POPULARITY. ATARI SOLD 150,000 UNITS OF HOME PONG IN THE GAME'S FIRST HOLIDAY SEASON. AND, THE COMPANY WOULD SOON REACH MILLIONS OF HOMES WITH ITS NEXT CONSOLE.
THE VIDEO GAMING INDUSTRY WAS BORN.

CHAPTER 2

THE DAWN OF VIDEO GAMES

IN 1975, MAGNAVOX'S ODYSSEY STOPPED
SELLING. BUT ATARI KEPT GROWING. IN
1977, IT RELEASED THE 2600, THEN KNOWN
AS THE VIDEO COMPUTER SYSTEM (VCS).

GAME CARTRIDGES AVAILABLE
INCLUDED NEW GAMES MADE
BY OTHER COMPANIES

JOYSTICKS GAVE PLAYERS MORE
CONTROL IN THEIR GAMES

PADDLE CONTROLLERS
TURNED LIKE DIALS TO
MOVE IN-GAME OBJECTS

THE ATARI 2600 SAW GREATER SUCCESS THAN THE ODYSSEY. SOME EXPERTS BELIEVE THIS WAS BECAUSE MAGNAVOX MARKETED THE ODYSSEY POORLY. ATARI MARKETED THE 2600 MORE EFFECTIVELY, AND MANY PEOPLE REGARDED ITS GAMES AS BEING OF BETTER QUALITY AND VARIETY.

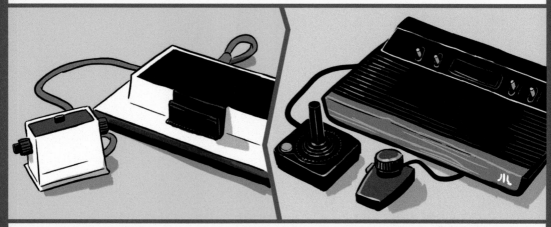

ATARI ALSO ALLOWED OTHER COMPANIES TO MAKE GAMES FOR THE 2600. THAT MEANT NEW OPTIONS FOR PLAYERS OVER TIME. THIS CHANGE HELPED VIDEO GAMING REALLY TAKE OFF.

MORE AND MORE GAMES HIT THE MARKET.

FROM 1977 TO 1992, COMPANIES RELEASED MORE THAN FIVE HUNDRED GAMES FOR THE 2600!

AMONG GAMES FOR THE ATARI, ONE STOOD OUT. SPACE INVADERS MADE THE 2600, AND VIDEO GAMING IN GENERAL, EVEN MORE POPULAR.

THE JAPANESE COMPANY TAITO DEVELOPED SPACE INVADERS AS AN ARCADE GAME IN 1978. THE COMPANY SOLD 300,000 SPACE INVADERS CABINETS WORLDWIDE.

IN 1980, TAITO RELEASED SPACE INVADERS FOR THE 2600. THE NUMBER OF 2600S IN US HOMES SOON DOUBLED TO TWO MILLION!

NEW HIGH SCORE!

NOT FOR LONG— MY TURN.

BEST 5

RANK	SCORE	ROUND	NAME
1ST	50000	5	LNR
2ND	40000	4	DHA
3RD	30000	3	HHH
4TH	20000	2	XXT
5TH	10000	1	OST

SPACE INVADERS WAS THE FIRST POPULAR HOME VIDEO GAME THAT ALLOWED USERS TO TRACK HIGH SCORES. PLAYERS LOVED THIS FEATURE.

THERE WERE NEARLY SIXTY THOUSAND CABINETS IN THE UNITED STATES ALONE.

THE SAME YEAR, ATARI RELEASED BATTLEZONE. ED ROTBERG CREATED THE GAME. IT WAS THE FIRST POPULAR VIDEO GAME TO LET PLAYERS MOVE AROUND IN A THREE-DIMENSIONAL WORLD.

BATTLEZONE

THE TECHNOLOGY BEHIND BATTLEZONE HAD USES BEYOND ENTERTAINMENT. THE US ARMY USED AN UPDATED VERSION OF THE GAME TO TRAIN VEHICLE DRIVERS.

IT'S LIKE DRIVING A TANK!

IT'S KIND OF LIKE DRIVING A TANK.

THE EARLY 1980S WERE A GREAT TIME FOR VIDEO GAMES. THEY'D NEVER BEEN BIGGER.

LET'S GOOOO!

MANY COMPANIES BEGAN MAKING GAMING CONSOLES. AND, MORE AND MORE GAMES WERE HITTING THE SHELVES. THE VIDEO GAME INDUSTRY WAS GROWING FAST . . .

COLECOVISION

ATARI 5200

ATARI 2600

INTELLIVISION

. . . TOO FAST. IN THE RUSH TO MAKE MONEY OFF THE VIDEO GAME CRAZE, SOME COMPANIES PUT OUT POORLY MADE GAMES.

$~~35~~ SALE $5!

NO, THANKS.

CUSTOMERS NOTICED.

14

AMONG THE GAMES THAT FLOPPED WAS E.T. THE EXTRA-TERRESTRIAL, MADE BY HOWARD SCOTT WARSHAW.

ATARI ONLY GAVE ME FIVE WEEKS TO MAKE E.T.! NORMALLY CREATORS HAVE SIX TO EIGHT MONTHS TO DESIGN A GAME, NOT FIVE WEEKS.

ATARI DIDN'T KNOW WHAT TO DO WITH THE GAMES THAT WOULDN'T SELL. IT ENDED UP BURYING MORE THAN 700,000 COPIES OF E.T. THE EXTRA-TERRESTRIAL AND OTHER GAMES IN A LANDFILL IN NEW MEXICO.

THE NORTH AMERICAN VIDEO GAME CRASH OF 1983 HAD BEGUN.

CHAPTER 3
CRASH & COMEBACK

IN 1983, ATARI SALES DROPPED, AND 1,500 VIDEO ARCADES SHUT DOWN ACROSS THE UNITED STATES.

I THOUGHT IT OPENED AT NOON?

I DON'T THINK IT'LL EVER BE OPEN AGAIN . . .

MANY PEOPLE WONDERED IF GAMING WAS DEAD AND GONE.

Nintendo®

BUT, A JAPANESE COMPANY WAS ABOUT TO BRING THE AMERICAN VIDEO GAMING INDUSTRY BACK TO LIFE.

MASAYUKI UEMURA WORKED FOR NINTENDO. HE DESIGNED ITS FAMILY COMPUTER GAMING SYSTEM, WHICH WAS POPULAR IN JAPAN.

MY WIFE CAME UP WITH THE NICKNAME "FAMICOM" FOR THE DEVICE.

MANY BUYERS REFERRED TO THE SYSTEM BY ITS NICKNAME. IN 1985, NINTENDO RELEASED THE CONSOLE IN THE UNITED STATES.

BUT IN THE UNITED STATES, NINTENDO CALLED FAMICOM THE NINTENDO ENTERTAINMENT SYSTEM (NES). THIS FOCUS ON ENTERTAINMENT SET THE CONSOLE APART FROM OTHER SYSTEMS.

NES GAME PACKAGING SHOWED WHAT GAMEPLAY LOOKED LIKE. PLAYERS COULD SEE THE GRAPHICS' QUALITY BEFORE BUYING THE GAME.

AND, NINTENDO'S GOAL WAS TO NEVER RUSH GAME DEVELOPMENT. NINTENDO DESIGNER SHIGERU MIYAMOTO UPHELD THIS GOAL.

A DELAYED GAME IS EVENTUALLY GOOD, BUT A RUSHED GAME IS FOREVER BAD.

NINTENDO'S BRANDING AND PHILOSOPHY HELPED IT STAND OUT FROM THE COMPETITION. SO DID ITS POPULAR CHARACTERS, SUCH AS THE HEROIC PLUMBER MARIO. GAMING SLOWLY CAME BACK.

IN 1989, JAPANESE COMPANY SEGA RELEASED A GAMING SYSTEM IN THE UNITED STATES: THE SEGA GENESIS.

THE GENESIS WAS A 16-BIT CONSOLE. THIS MEANS IT COULD TRANSFER SIXTEEN BITS, OR PIECES OF DATA, AT A TIME. THE NES WAS AN 8-BIT CONSOLE.

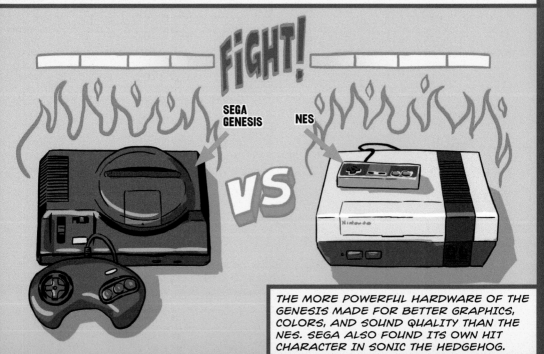

THE MORE POWERFUL HARDWARE OF THE GENESIS MADE FOR BETTER GRAPHICS, COLORS, AND SOUND QUALITY THAN THE NES. SEGA ALSO FOUND ITS OWN HIT CHARACTER IN SONIC THE HEDGEHOG.

STILL, BETWEEN ITS 1985 RELEASE AND THE MID-1990S, THE NES SOLD TWICE AS MANY CONSOLES AS GENESIS IN THE UNITED STATES.

IS IT MY TURN YET?

NOPE! I JUST GOT AN EXTRA LIFE!

SOME HISTORIANS BELIEVE NINTENDO GAMES WERE MORE TIMELESS AND SEGA GAMES MORE TRENDY. THIS MAY BE WHY THE NES SOLD BETTER OVER THE TWO CONSOLES' LIFETIMES.

THE COMPETITION MADE BOTH COMPANIES WORK TO IMPROVE THEIR PRODUCTS. IT ALSO INSPIRED OTHER COMPANIES TO CREATE COOL NEW GAMING SYSTEMS.

OOOH!

MINE!

THE CONSOLE WARS HAD BEGUN.

COOL!

THE CONSOLE WARS!

COMPETING COMPANIES BEGAN MAKING FASTER, MORE POWERFUL GAMING SYSTEMS. EACH GENERATION OF CONSOLES WAS BETTER THAN THE LAST. BETWEEN 1991 AND 2001, VIDEO GAME COMPANIES SOLD MORE THAN TWO MILLION GAMING SYSTEMS IN THE UNITED STATES ALONE.

SONY PLAYSTATION

RELEASED: 1995
KEY FEATURE: 32-BIT GRAPHICS
SALES: 30.4 MILLION UNITS

SUPER NINTENDO ENTERTAINMENT SYSTEM (SNES)

RELEASED: 1991
KEY FEATURE: 16-BIT GRAPHICS
SALES: 20 MILLION UNITS

NINTENDO 64

RELEASED: 1996
KEY FEATURE: 64-BIT GRAPHICS
SALES: 18 MILLION UNITS

SONY PLAYSTATION 2

RELEASED: 2000
KEY FEATURE: 128-BIT GRAPHICS
SALES: 46.4 MILLION UNITS

SEGA DREAMCAST

RELEASED: 1999
KEY FEATURE: 128-BIT GRAPHICS
SALES: 4.1 MILLION UNITS

MICROSOFT XBOX

RELEASED: NOVEMBER 15, 2001
KEY FEATURE: LAUNCHED THE
POPULAR HALO GAME SERIES
SALES: 14.5 MILLION UNITS

NINTENDO GAMECUBE

RELEASED: NOVEMBER 18, 2001
KEY FEATURE: CUBE-LIKE DESIGN
SALES: 11.8 MILLION UNITS

VIDEO GAME WARS DIDN'T JUST OCCUR OVER SALES. SEVERAL GAMES EARNED NEGATIVE ATTENTION FOR THEIR GRAPHIC VIOLENCE. ONE WAS MORTAL KOMBAT, RELEASED IN THE EARLY 1990S.

TAKE THAT!

ARGHHH! YOU GOT ME!

PARENTS AND PUBLIC FIGURES WORRIED. THEY THOUGHT VIDEO GAME VIOLENCE MIGHT LEAD PLAYERS TO BECOME VIOLENT IN REAL LIFE. IN 1993, US SENATOR JOE LIEBERMAN SPOKE AGAINST VIOLENT VIDEO GAMES.

FEW PARENTS WOULD BUY THESE GAMES FOR THEIR KIDS IF THEY KNEW WHAT WAS IN THEM.

IN 1994, THE VIDEO GAME INDUSTRY REACTED TO THE OUTCRY. IT CREATED THE ENTERTAINMENT SOFTWARE RATING BOARD (ESRB).

MOM, MOM! CAN I GET IT?!

MAYBE IN A FEW YEARS. YOU'RE TOO YOUNG FOR THAT ONE.

THE ESRB RATES VIDEO GAMES AS SUITED FOR CERTAIN AGES. THE VIDEO GAME INDUSTRY CONTINUES TO USE THESE RATINGS.

MEANWHILE, WARS WERE ALSO RAGING IN THE COMPUTER WORLD. BILL GATES HAD COFOUNDED MICROSOFT. STEVE JOBS HAD COFOUNDED APPLE. THEIR COMPETING VISIONS CHANGED PERSONAL COMPUTERS.

BILL GATES

COMPUTERS SHOULD BE CUSTOMIZABLE AND POWERFUL.

COMPUTERS SHOULD BE SIMPLE AND STYLISH.

STEVE JOBS

FIGHT!

IN THE 1990S, PERSONAL COMPUTERS BECAME MORE COMMON IN AMERICAN HOUSEHOLDS. COMPUTER GAMING ALSO BECAME POPULAR. COMPUTERS EVOLVED IN WAYS GAMING CONSOLES COULDN'T.

WHAT DOES THIS PART DO?

VIDEO GAME CONSOLE HARDWARE COULDN'T BE UPGRADED. INSTEAD, CONSOLE MAKERS HAD TO RELEASE NEW DEVICES. COMPUTERS, ON THE OTHER HAND, COULD HAVE NEW PARTS INSTALLED. THIS ALLOWED ADVANCED GAMING OPTIONS WITHOUT HAVING TO REPLACE A DEVICE!

MANY PEOPLE LOVED TINKERING WITH COMPUTERS.

I JUST UPGRADED MY OLD HARD DRIVE TO A SOLID STATE ONE! AND THIS NEW THERMAL PASTE SHOULD LET ME OVERCLOCK MY CPU WITHOUT MAKING IT OVERHEAT . . .

HOWEVER, COMPUTERS WERE MORE EXPENSIVE TOO. SO, MANY GAMERS CONTINUED TO PREFER CONSOLES.

CHAPTER 4

PORTABLE & MULTIPLAYER

AS DEVICES AND TECHNOLOGY CONTINUED TO ADVANCE, GAMING DREW IN PLAYERS FROM ALL WALKS OF LIFE . . .

ONE MAJOR INNOVATION WAS PORTABLE GAMING. SEVERAL HANDHELD GAMING DEVICES WERE LAUNCHED IN THE 1980S. IN 1989, NINTENDO DEBUTED THE GAME BOY. IT WAS VERY POPULAR!

NINTENDO RELEASED MANY VERSIONS OF THE GAME BOY IN THE FOLLOWING YEARS. OTHER COMPANIES, INCLUDING PLAYSTATION AND SEGA, ALSO MADE PORTABLE CONSOLES.

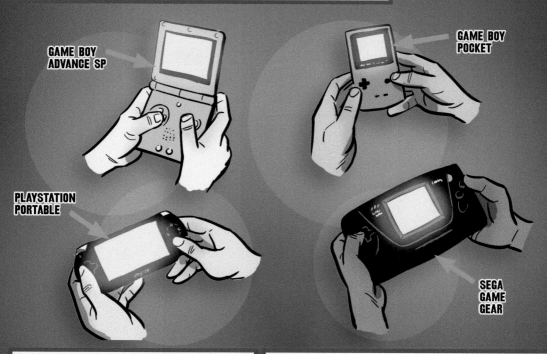

GAME BOY ADVANCE SP

GAME BOY POCKET

PLAYSTATION PORTABLE

SEGA GAME GEAR

IN THE TWENTY-FIRST CENTURY, SMARTPHONES BECAME INCREASINGLY POPULAR. THESE DEVICES TOOK PORTABLE GAMING TO A NEW LEVEL. IT WAS LIKE HAVING A MINI COMPUTER ON THE GO!

WE'RE HERE, KAI. DON'T FORGET YOUR BACKPACK!

MEANWHILE, NINTENDO KEPT INNOVATING. IN 2017, IT MADE THE NINTENDO SWITCH.

A GAMER CAN PLAY THE SWITCH AS A PORTABLE SYSTEM OR PLUG IT DIRECTLY INTO A TV AS A HOME CONSOLE.

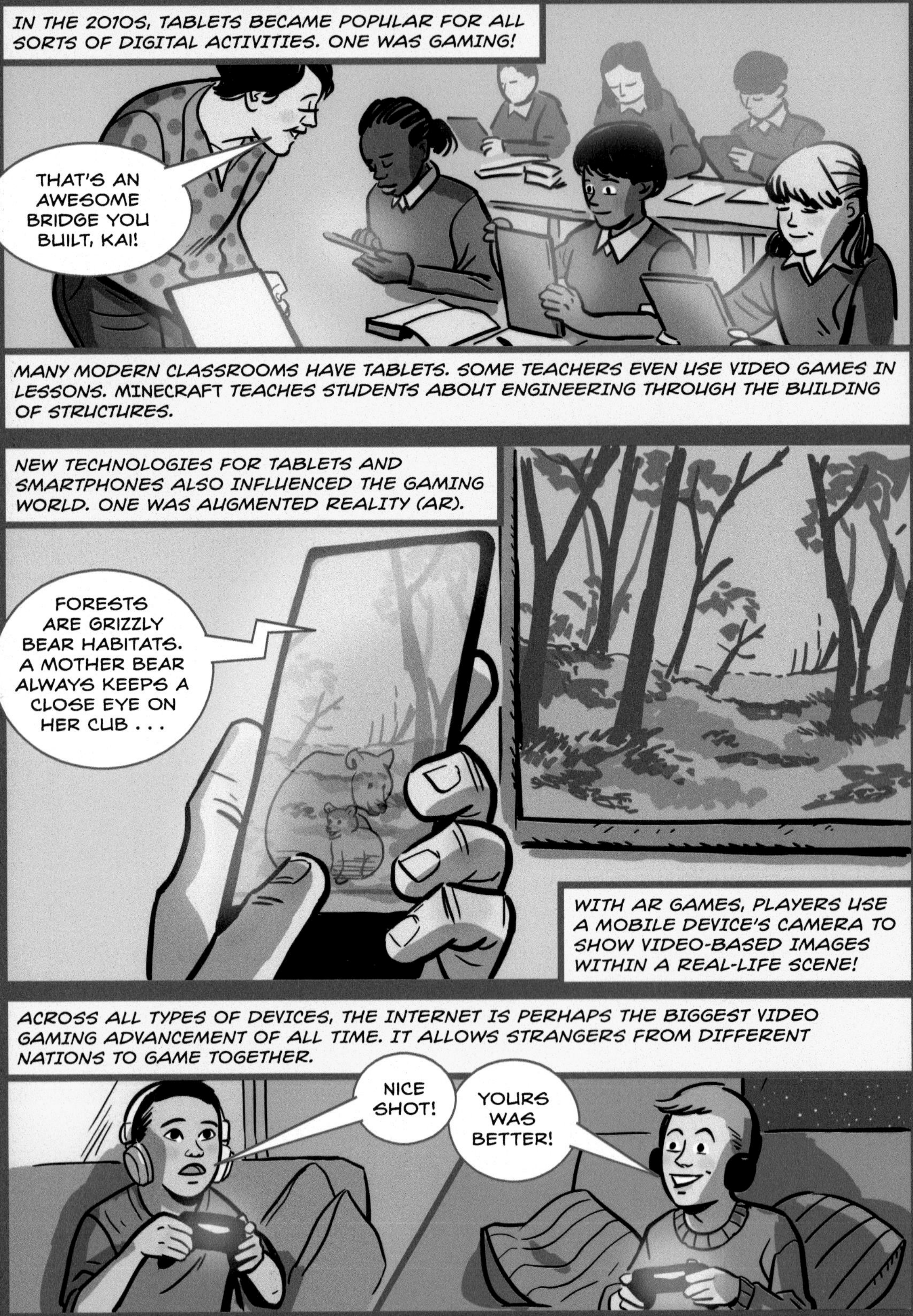
IN THE 2010S, TABLETS BECAME POPULAR FOR ALL SORTS OF DIGITAL ACTIVITIES. ONE WAS GAMING!
THAT'S AN AWESOME BRIDGE YOU BUILT, KAI!
MANY MODERN CLASSROOMS HAVE TABLETS. SOME TEACHERS EVEN USE VIDEO GAMES IN LESSONS. MINECRAFT TEACHES STUDENTS ABOUT ENGINEERING THROUGH THE BUILDING OF STRUCTURES.
NEW TECHNOLOGIES FOR TABLETS AND SMARTPHONES ALSO INFLUENCED THE GAMING WORLD. ONE WAS AUGMENTED REALITY (AR).
FORESTS ARE GRIZZLY BEAR HABITATS. A MOTHER BEAR ALWAYS KEEPS A CLOSE EYE ON HER CUB . . .
WITH AR GAMES, PLAYERS USE A MOBILE DEVICE'S CAMERA TO SHOW VIDEO-BASED IMAGES WITHIN A REAL-LIFE SCENE!
ACROSS ALL TYPES OF DEVICES, THE INTERNET IS PERHAPS THE BIGGEST VIDEO GAMING ADVANCEMENT OF ALL TIME. IT ALLOWS STRANGERS FROM DIFFERENT NATIONS TO GAME TOGETHER.
NICE SHOT!
YOURS WAS BETTER!

MULTIPLAYER VIDEO GAMES ARE MODERN MARVELS.

ONLY THIRTEEN PLAYERS LEFT.

PEOPLE PLAY WITH AND AGAINST HUNDREDS OF PLAYERS AT ONCE!

DOWN TO THE FINAL SEVEN . . .

THESE GAMES CONNECT PLAYERS ACROSS THE WORLD FOR FUN AND COMPETITION.

I GOT THIRD PLACE!

YOU WON!

I WON! I WON!

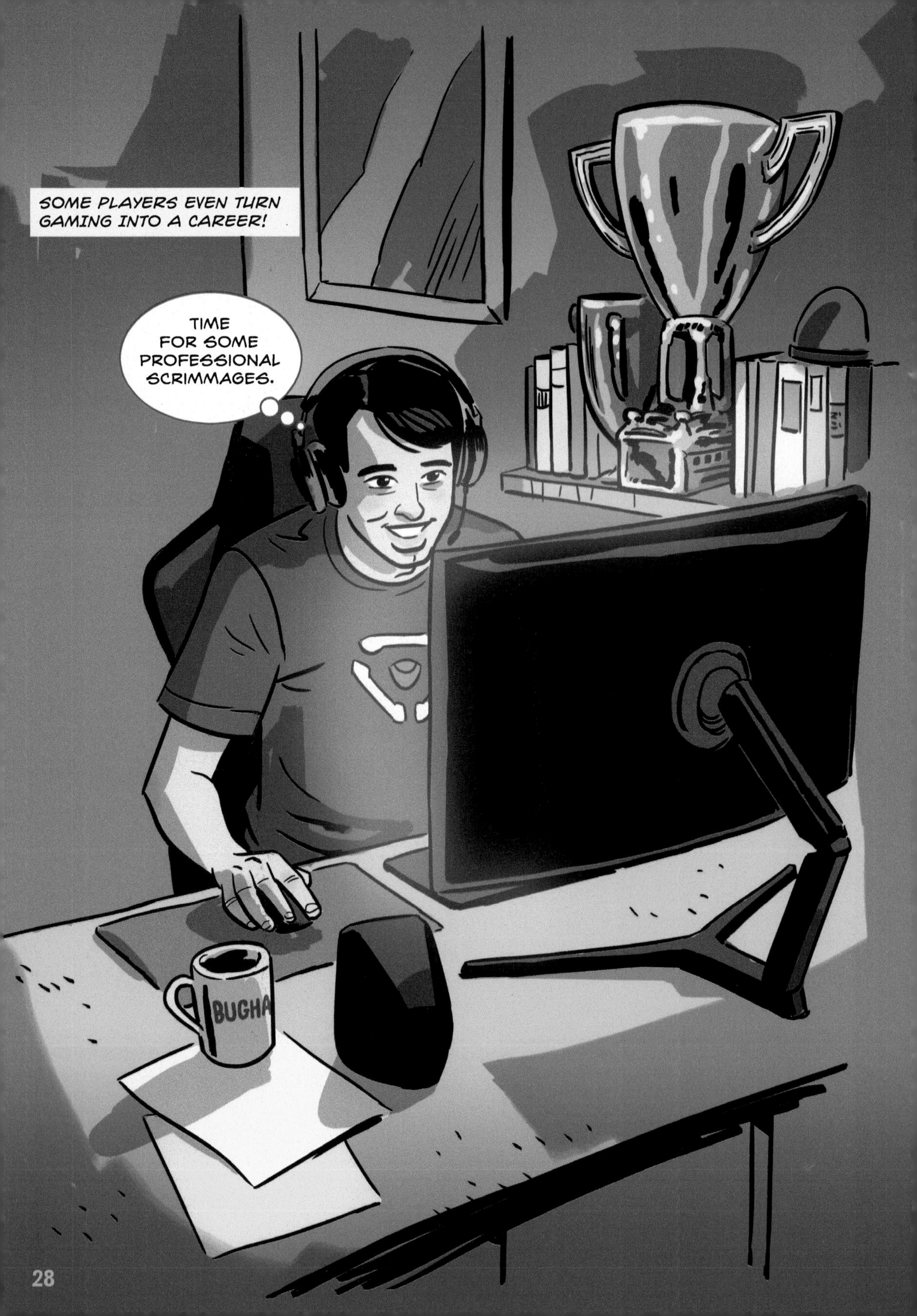
SOME PLAYERS EVEN TURN GAMING INTO A CAREER!
TIME FOR SOME PROFESSIONAL SCRIMMAGES.
BUGHA

SOURCE NOTES

PAGE 5

Tsukuyama, Hayley. "Video Game Designer Ralph Baer Invented Your Childhood." https://www.washingtonpost.com/news /the-switch/wp/2014/12/08/video-game -designer-ralph-baer-invented-your-childhood -here-are-five-things-you-can-learn-from-his -extraordinary-life/. December 8th, 2014.

PAGE 15

1. Lamble, Ryan. "Howard Scott Warshaw on Creating E.T. and Atari: Game Over." https://www.denofgeek.com/games /howard-scott-warshaw/33708/howard -scott-warshaw-on-creating-et-and-atari -game-over. January 21, 2015.

2. Hooper, Richard. "The Man Who Made 'the Worst Video Game in History'." https://www.bbc.com/news/magazine -35560458. February 22, 2016.

PAGE 17

1. Blaster, Master. "Famicom Creator Masayuki Uemura Had No Faith in the Game System's Success, Colored It after His Boss' Scarf." https://soranews24.com /2013/04/30/famicom-creator-masayuki -uemura-had-no-faith-in-the-game-systems -success-colored-it-after-his-boss-scarf/. April 30, 2013.

2. Seedhouse, Alex. "Shigeru Miyamoto Reflects On His Most Famous Quote." https://www.nintendo-insider.com/shigeru -miyamoto-reflects-on-his-most-famous -quote/. April 10, 2016.

PAGE 22

Crossley, Rob. "Mortal Kombat: Violent Game that Changed Video Games Industry." https://www.bbc.com/news/technology -27620071/. June 2, 2014.

PAGE 23

Kapko, Matt. "History of Apple and Microsoft: 4 Decades of Peaks and Valleys." https://www.cio.com/article/2989667/history -of-apple-and-microsoft-4-decades-of-peaks -and-valleys.html/. October 7, 2015.

GLOSSARY

ARCADE: a business with machines for amusement, such as video games, which customers pay to play

CARTRIDGE: a plastic case containing software. A cartridge is inserted into a console to run a video game.

CONSOLE: an electronic system that connects to a display and is used to play video games

CONTROVERSY: an argument in which people express strongly opposing views about something

EVOLVE: to develop and change as a result of many small steps

INDUSTRY: a single branch of business or trade

JOYSTICK: a lever that can be moved in several directions to control movement in a video game

PORTABLE: able to be easily carried or moved from place to place

SCRIMMAGE: a practice game in team sports

LEARN MORE

Beanz—History of Video Games.
www.kidscodecs.com/video-game-history/

Hansen, Dustin. *Game On! Video Game History from Pong and Pac-Man to Mario, Minecraft, and More*. New York: Feiwel & Friends, 2016.

Kaplan, Arie. *The Inner Workings of Video Games*. Minneapolis: Lerner Publications, 2014.

Lyons, Heather. *Programming Games and Animation*. Minneapolis: Lerner Publications, 2017.

Stevens, Cara J. *The Ultimate Unofficial Encyclopedia for Minecrafters, Multiplayer Mode: Discovering Hidden Games and Secret Worlds*. New York: Skyhorse Publishing, 2017.

The Strong National Museum of Play—Video Game History Timeline
https://www.museumofplay.org/about/icheg/video-game-history/timeline

INDEX